Through Our Eyes

Voices
from the Campus
of Burlington United Methodist
Family Services, Inc.
Burlington, WV

International Standard Book Number 0-87012-668-7
Library of Congress Control Number 2001095494
Printed in the United States of America
Copyright © 2001 by Burlington United Methodist Church
Burlington, WV
All Rights Reserved
2001

McClain Printing Company
Parsons, WV
www.mcclainprinting.com

*"I am about to do
a new thing;
now it springs forth,
do you not perceive it?"*
Isaiah 43: 19

Table of Contents

Preface	
The Vision	1-3
Faith	4-22
Friends	23-33
Family	34-46
Feelings	47-94
Future	95-102
Appendix	103-125

Preface

This book you are holding is a kind of miracle—honestly. Imagine a group of at-risk youth, desiring to have a chapel of their own in which to worship and develop their faith, wanting to help get funds to build it, being willing to reveal their innermost thoughts and feelings in the process, and giving up their free time in the evening to come to class to do so. Amazing, isn't it? Yes, it is—and thankfully so!!

In the process of compiling this book, we literally dealt with a handful of issues——five of them: faith, friends, family, feelings, and the future. Those became the divisions in our book. Aren't those five areas the ones that all of us must analyze and understand in order to be successful in our lives? At-risk youth are no different. When asked to give us insight into their lives and of youth today, they did so willingly——with maturity and sensitivity. We are greatly indebted to them for their efforts.

"....and a little child shall lead them."
Isaiah 11:6

The Youth Had A Vision...

Burlington United Methodist Family Services, Inc., is a residential care treatment facility for at-risk youth from ages ten years to those in transitional living, which can be until age twenty-one. The youth are here resulting from a wide spectrum of challenges ranging from truancy to abuse or a combination of factors where parental rights have been terminated. After being placed on a referral list by a social worker and being accepted for placement on our campus, the residents are grouped in housing units where staff supervision simulates family living as closely as possible: the youth have chores to do, cook for the unit, help with cleaning, are responsible for their room, have family-style dinners, and are given summer jobs to earn money for clothes and vacation, etc.—all the responsibilities and activities one would expect in a normally-functioning family. In conjunction with that, support services such as group and individual counseling, medical needs, and behavioral and educational concerns are addressed. An important aspect of their life as part of our program is their spiritual growth. That duty—such activities as the entrance interview and giving out Bibles when they begin the program, regular Christian education classes, planning holiday worship services, and group and individual counseling——falls to our campus chaplain, Rev. Angela Cosner. Rev. Cosner serves as chaplain and friend in time of crisis to staff as well as the youth in addition to heading the campus Spiritual Life Committee.

Staff and employees—past and present—have often talked of having a campus chapel, but the vision to actively seek the building of a campus chapel and to help finance the effort was born in the minds of the youth during a discussion of a resident council meeting. In resident council, they are encouraged to voice opinions and work to become part of the total campus ministry. The resident council is a leadership team begun by Pastor Cosner consisting of two residents and one staff person from each of the five units of the campus. The group meets monthly and is intended to allow the residents to have input and representation in campus affairs and, thus, feel more connection and ownership of campus events.

They had discussed wanting a campus chapel at resident council meetings before, and the desire had been growing within them. The time had come to make their wishes known! The vision had been formed, and the wheels were beginning to turn! The idea was well-received, and the administration decided to proceed with plans.

After learning that the chapel project would be started, their excitement ignited and the residents wanted to support it. They began to seek a project that would allow them to do their part and contribute to the building fund. Pastor Angela had recently published a book of faith stories, and they began asking about the process. Gradually a plan was beginning to formulate——with her help, **they** could put together a collection of writings, also.

The residents and the administration are well aware of the holistic therapy of writing. It is a time-proven way to promote growth and healing in young and old alike, so it was decided that a creative arts class would be offered on campus, and the work from the class would be published into a book. Proceeds from the sales would be donated to the chapel building fund.

Pastor Angela and Kathy Johnson, a volunteer and teacher friend with whom she had written and published her book, began meeting with the residents during evening sessions and compiling the material.

Our campus is richly blessed by having a supportive, hard-working auxiliary that whole-heartedly participates in the campus ministry, making much of what we do possible. The idea was presented to the group with samples of the writings, and they enthusiastically agreed to support the book idea. The auxiliary would provide the funds needed for publication!! An exciting project—a powerful witness tool which would help make our campus chapel possible—would be a reality.

This book—another goal and vision of our youth——is a collection of the writing, discussion, group work, and individual assignments from the residents as they have responded to writing prompts and the group activities during our creative arts class. Some of the work is typically teenage, and some of it is very profound. Through it all, one can sense the gamut of emotions that the youth feel and get some insight into how they deal with the daily struggles they encounter. What results is an honest, sometimes very somber depiction of teenage life which some of us have forgotten and many of us have never experienced. In much of the writing and responses, a very evident thread of faith and hope is found. That is a testament to the total campus ministry here at Burlington——and to the administration, the staff, and the army of volunteers that make our success possible!

"Be ye strong therefore, and let not your hands be weak:
for your work shall be rewarded."
2 Chronicles 15:7

Creative Arts Class

Our Vision Begins…....

Chaplain Angela Cosner setting our goal, going over the blueprint for the new chapel——our vision becoming reality!

Thinking——writing——talking--sharing——Every meeting adds more pages and more memories!

Relaxing after class— snacking— laughing — talking—

Faith

*"Now faith is the substance
of things hoped for,
the evidence of things
not seen."
Hebrews 11:1*

Faith
GroupThink

Faith is a rainbow that never ends.

Life is an adventure worth exploring.

Life is a book that never ends.

Faith is a dinnerplate in the buffet of life.

Faith is a gift that anyone can receive.

Faith is like a gentle breeze—you can't see it, but you can feel it.

Faith is like a baby——it has to be nurtured and fed.

Burlington is a harbor that provides rest for its travelers.

Life is a book that needs to be opened.

Faith is like sunshine on a cloudy day.

Faith is an umbrella in the storms of life.

Life is like a movie that always has a sequel.

Witnessing and Sharing God's Love

"Happiness is having God in your life because He makes all miracles in your life come true."
                                   Elizabeth

"If I could be or do anything in this world, I would help everyone with everything and tell them all about God.
I am a firm believer in the Bible, and even though I choose to do the wrong things at times, I just take everyday as a fresh start to get back on my feet and start over."
                                   Oneda

"God is an angel that is in heaven, a king that rules the good people like me. God is beautiful, like a shining silver unicorn with a golden horn that He uses to fight for us and protect us from danger. I love God so much."

"God is love that is deep in my heart; God is wisdom that we have sitting in us. God roars like a mighty lion when it thunders and cries when it rains. God is a shield that is there when we need protection. God is a father that is there when we need Him. God is everything."
                                   Kristal

"When I went on a missionary trip to Chicago in 1998, I went door-to-door witnessing. A lady had gotten saved and she became a steady member at our old pastor's church in Chicago."
                              Oneda

God
(His Love for us)

It's listening to me as I ramble—
Being there to catch me as I fall,
Never using my heart to gamble—
Always beside me at my beck and call.

It's the echoes of laughter,
The warmth I feel in His arms.
It strengthens as we grow together—
He knows my weaknesses and my charms.

It flows deep within my soul—
Making my days easier to endure.
It protects me by night, making me whole—
Giving me peace, making me secure.

It is unconditional and always true—
He feels these things in His love for you.

Elizabeth

Bow Your Head

Bow your head and begin to pray
about all the things
you need in your life today.
Bow your head and thank God
for all he's done
because of the victory He has won.
Bow your head and think of the things you can do
Because the one He loves is <u>You</u>!

Oneda

More Than Once

More than once
I put you
back on that cross....
Another nail in your hand,
a spear in your side.
More than once have
I called your name
Oh Lord, Dear God.
But I am ashamed,
for it's been in vain.
All you asked is for unconditional love
And I give you my all...
But only when it's convenient for me.
More than once has a cruel word
Rolled off my tongue.
Take away this hate
And replace it with your love.
More than once I've awakened
With a good view of the day ahead.
But I forgot to ask for help
And failed instead.
More than once have I sinned,
Then asked for your forgiveness.
You forgive lovingly and with a smile,
For you say I am your child.
More than once have you given me
A second chance
And I thank you...
More than once.

This hauntingly-honest poem was written for Pastor Angie and given to her by one of the residents in her Christian Education classes.

Gratitude and Thanks

"I am grateful for my family, my health, and my faith in God to be able to live each day with faith and joy……"

"I feel grateful for the help Burlington's given me. I used to go off really easy, then I had to be restrained. I have learned to trust my staff and walk away from angry talk. I've also learned to take control of my life."
Kristal

"I am grateful for what I have accomplished and what I have now."
Crystal

"I am grateful for my family, God, and Jesus; being alive; my friends; the support system I have; having a place to stay such as Craig House; raising my siblings; getting taken out of my home before things got any worse; people who care about me."
Oneda

"I feel grateful for making something out of myself. When I was a small child, I was poor and never got the things I wanted. I wasn't that great at school, and I was always dirty. I think something told me I needed better than that, and that is why I told the truth about everything. As I started getting older, I learned new things like how to be a better person. Since I was placed at BUMFS, which was four years ago, I have changed. I am just a better person. I feel good about myself—period!"
Leeann

A Rose

Each petal represents
A portion of our life;
A chapter in which
We learn
We grow.

The fragrance is the truth
Within us.
The branches tell of
Reaching out
To catch our dreams.

The color is the laughter
We shared.
The dew, the tears.
The roots are the
Strength we gained.
The softness is the wisdom
We have come to know.

Jackie

Are There
Angels Among Us?

I believe an angel is a guidance and a person who stands by your side and you can count on to lean on. Also, they help answer your prayers. Angels come from a place called the Golden Throne. Angels look like the most beautiful women and men in the world. Their clothing is the neatest and the cleanest.
                Tanganika

How do we know angels exist?
"The night I was saved, I saw an angel!"

I believe the form of an angel is completely unknown
to our human sight.
Blue eyes, blonde hair. Tall, skinny. Who knows?
These they might.
Some are assigned to a different destiny.
There's one to help you and one to help me.
They don't do the things that we wish they could do,
It's not their job. They just try to guide me and you.
I believe that everyone has one special angel around.
Some people will never know—
'cause they'll never hear a sound.
But even though we have different guardians
watching over our heads,
We still pray to the "Big Man"
when we go to bed.
                Nikki

Angels are there to protect the living.
They come from Heaven.
They look like a human,
But they have wings.
Angels are always around.
      Valleri

Angels are vibrant and beautiful.
——they are out there,
   here or somewhere.
Everyone has a guardian angel that protects us
    and makes us feel calm.
 We believe their presence is around us
       Each and every day!
  Karissa

Angels are here and angels are there.
We believe they are out there somewhere.
We believe they surround us with protection and help.
We recognize them because their presence is around.
Each and every person has a guardian angel.
They come from Heaven up above.
When they help us, it's because they love.
Their wings are sensational and beautiful...and
  they make us feel vibrant and calm.
      Oneda

Angels

I believe....
Angels——everyone has one nearby.
Angels——have feathers on the form of a human and spirit.
Angels——are there to protect the living.
Angels——yes, I think I have one around.
Angels——come from Heaven.
Elizabeth

An angel is there when you need him or her to help you with troubles. An angel sometimes steps in and prevents a tragedy from happening to us. Angels whisper sweet thoughts into our heads and push the bad thoughts out. If we have faith, our guardian angel will always protect us. An angel can take on any form it needs to. An angel is a messenger from God.
Everyone has an angel, but some choose not to listen. They follow the devil instead.
Lisa

Angel
I believe an angel is a spirit we can't see,
helping us every day,
leading us through the day
and showing us the way.
I believe that my angel
is my grandfather and he's here to stay.
Crystal

Angels…..

"Some people don't believe in God because they can't see Him. Some people don't believe in angels because they can't see them, either."
   Leeann

Angels
The form is a person with wings.
They come from Heaven.
They wear a white dress.
I think I have an angel with me.
I feel that they are there.
I believe they protect me.
I know they exist because I believe in them.
I believe that my great-great grandma is an angel.
   Kristal

Angels are heavenly sent,
To every woman, man, and child.
The wings of an angel hold us close
Trying to make us feel worthwhile.
   Teresa

An Angel is someone who...

Always listens to us,

   Nurtures us and

      Gives willingly to us,

         Encouraging each of us to

            Love one another and

               Set worthwhile goals for ourselves.

This poem was written by a young woman to describe the experience she felt the night she was saved. When one reads it with that in mind, it is powerfully moving and inspiring!

Angel Kisses

Softly but sweetly,
I was touched by the lips of an angel.
At first, I was scared and shivers covered my body.
Was I dreaming or was I really filled with laughter
like never before?
The angel slowly came near me
And I was blinded by the beautiful glow of her wings.
The angel happened to look transparent.
She was sensational, almost imperceptible.
The kiss was so soft and overwhelming
I thought I was floating in mid-air.
She kissed my cheek like a radiant bride
Going to meet her groom.
For an instant,
I thought I was more powerful than any other.
I then realized
That my life was changed forever
By the kiss of an angel!
From that point on,
I felt as if I were set free!

Oneda

Some thoughts
on
Baptism...

"I feel that baptism means I dedicated my life to God as His child born unto Him."
Crystal

"When I get baptized, I think I will be a better person. I would like to be baptized and my soul cleansed."
Matt

"I think baptism is where you get closer to God and you see a different life."
Becky

"Baptism is believing in God and getting dunked in water and seeing a new life."
Leeann

"You have to be baptized in the name of the Father, the Son, and the Holy Spirit. You have to believe in Jesus Christ, and you have to have a pure heart."
Chris

"I might have been baptized as an infant, but I don't remember. I would like to learn more about baptism and its importance in my life."   Tim

"I have never been baptized, but I have the desire to be because Jesus set the example. I have Jesus in my heart, and I want the world to know."
      Marco

"(Being baptized means)...my life was dedicated to Christ, I understand Him in my life, and I committed myself to Him."
      Valleri

"It's an outward sign to show your dedication to God."

"....belief of love for God. You are willing to get rid of all your sins for a new beginning."
      Teresa

"...the rebirth of your Christian faith, an outward sign of your inward emotions."

"I think that baptism means when you first meet the Lord. It's a day when you go into the water and pray and ask God to reveal Jesus to the world."
      Mark

"I believe baptism is scary. I think when I go under the water, I will drown. If I go under the water, I will become a better person. God will protect me and save me from mean people."   Trevor

"...buried in the likeness of His death, born into the resurrection of His Savior when you're ready to show you've accepted God as your Savior."
                              Toshia

"...a rebirth of your faith in God, a conscious awareness of right and wrong, a new birth on God's path."

"If I were baptized, I would expect God to take my body and soul and show me the right way."
                              Roy

"I have not been saved by baptism, but I was saved on January 16 at 6:30 P.M., and I felt great after I asked God into my heart, to ask God in for a long visit, and to thank Him and praise Him…"   Jason

"I think I am ready to be baptized….."
                              Kristal

"Baptism is something you do to show others your commitment to Christ. To be sure of yourself, you should go under with a grateful heart……I was baptized when I was twelve years old."
                              Oneda

"Baptism is a time to be accepted by your faith. I have not yet been accepted by being baptized, but I do want to be baptized. I want that sense of the feeling of worthiness, control over my heart and soul over my faith. This is a time of rebirth of my faith. When you're truly baptized, your whole life will have a clean feeling, for you do clean your soul…"
                              Nikki

About Giving And Serving....

*Campus residents actively participate in worship services and other functions. The following are messages that have been written and shared by residents during services or at Apple Harvest. The wisdom and insight presented in them are touching—then **and** now!*

Lectionary text: Matthew 28:16-20

God has a plan for our lives. Each of us is used in God's own way to spread his message. Some of us do it by drawing, singing, acting, or speaking. Either way you spread the Word, you are a disciple for Christ.

God wants us to talk of His loving kindness and how easy it is to be forgiven of sin. God uses our special talents to bring people to Him. Being a disciple is not that easy, though. Every day as Christians, we are criticized and made fun of. People expect us to be as perfect as Christ was. We are sinful by nature. We will never be as Christ was on Earth.

Now, even though there are drawbacks to being a disciple, there are many rewards. By telling others of Christ, we hopefully encourage them to follow Him. And knowing that you did what God wanted you to do, by bringing back a lost lamb, gives you a feeling of achievement and pleasure.

I enjoy speaking to people about Christ because it brings me back to reality and helps me get back on track with life. I say this because I still struggle with problems from the past that are being thrown up in my face by Satan. I hope that I have encouraged some of you to go out and spread God's message even more.

Jay

"Go ye therefore, and teach all nations…
Teaching them to observe all things whatsoever I have commanded you…
…I am with you always, even unto the end of the world."

Overcoming Temptation

We as Christians are tempted every day. Satan fills our minds with lust, hatred, greed, gangs, war, sex, theft, drugs, and thoughts of owning worldly possessions. In Luke Chapter 4, Christ gives us things to say to rebuke Satan and gives us other ideas on how to put down Satan. We are all imperfect beings and sinners, but if we follow Christ's example and read our Bibles, we will become stronger than Satan and will be able to rebuke him with ease. To be able to do so, we must ask Christ our Lord into our hearts and pray for His wisdom and guidance. Then we will be able to follow Christ's example. God lets us know in the Bible that if we are down and troubled, pray to him and he will help us.

One night a man had a dream. He dreamed he was walking along the beach with the Lord. Across the sky flashed scenes from his life. For each scene, he noticed two sets of footprints in the sand: one belonging to him, and the other to the Lord.

When the last scene of his life flashed before him, he looked back at the footprints in the sand. He noticed that many times along the path of his life, there was only one set of footprints. He also noticed that it happened at the very lowest and saddest times in his life.

This really bothered him, and he questioned the Lord about it. "Lord, you said that once I decided to follow you, you'd walk with me all the way. But I have noticed that during the most troublesome times in my life, there is only one set of footprints. I don't understand why when I needed you most, you would leave me." The Lord replied, "My son, My precious child, I love you, and I would never leave you. During your times of trial and suffering, when you see only one set of footprints, it was then that I carried you."

Many times I have been tempted with past behaviors. I prayed to God, and I was able to overcome. So for those of you who have not asked Christ into your life, please pray to Christ and invite Him into your heart.

Dear Heavenly Father,
We ask that you fill us with your strength and
wisdom to overcome temptation. We are weak, Lord,
but through you we can be strong. Lord, we thank you
for showing us how to be a good Christian. We ask again
that you be with us each day to help us resist everyday
temptations. We ask this in the name of Jesus Christ,
Amen

Jeff

The Magic of a Miracle

A volunteer is one who does something for one person or groups of people of their own free will without pay or reward—*one who makes miracles happen.* It takes a special person, regardless of age, to be a volunteer.

Christ is a good example of a volunteer who made miracles happen every day. One way he acted as a volunteer and made a miracle happen was when he gave up his personal relaxing time to teach the crowds, even though he was tired of teaching at that time and wanted to relax. The Bible tells us that story in Mark 6: 35-44.

People were hungry and one young boy, a volunteer, gave of his lunch so that every one could be fed. Volunteers give of what they have. For some, that isn't much material-wise, but to give a little and love a lot is what makes a volunteer special.

God also said in the Bible that he who gives what he honestly can and does it with a loving heart will be graciously rewarded…. those who have volunteered their services and expected nothing in return.

Because of volunteers, I have the opportunity to succeed in life. I am grateful for their love and kindness. They have inspired me to volunteer my free time….. as a way to give back what was given to me.

God loves us all,
and he uses the special volunteers
to change other people's lives.
To God, all volunteers are special.
Jay

Friends

"A friend loveth
at all times...."
Proverbs 17:17

Friends
GroupThink

Friends are the desserts of life.

A friend is a flower that blooms every day.

Friends are the shade of a blistery day.

A friend is a gem that sparkles and gleams.

A good friend is a Porsche on the road of life.

A friend is a treasure that you keep closely guarded.

True friends are like treasure—they are hard to find.

A best friend is like bubble gum—it sticks no matter what.

A friend is a teddy bear that needs to be cared for.

Friends are a shelter in a dark, scary storm.

A friend is the mirage in the desert of life.

Friends are the family that you get to pick for yourself.

A friend is a rainstorm on a hot, muggy day.

The following was turned in one evening by a youth during our creative arts class. It was not part of a class assignment, but a genuine effort to express gratitude for what she has experienced during her placement at Burlington. It serves as a testimony of the youth's maturity, sharing so honestly, and to the staff's dedication, who give so freely.

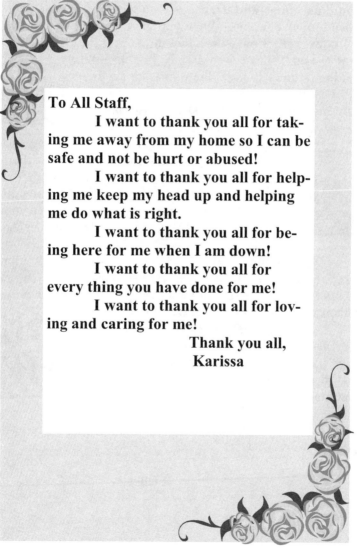

To All Staff,

    I want to thank you all for taking me away from my home so I can be safe and not be hurt or abused!

    I want to thank you all for helping me keep my head up and helping me do what is right.

    I want to thank you all for being here for me when I am down!

    I want to thank you all for every thing you have done for me!

    I want to thank you all for loving and caring for me!

               Thank you all,
                Karissa

Show of Hands

...I have a fetish for hands and feet, especially hands. In my paintings and drawings I do with my counselor, they mostly involve hands. When you gave this paper to do, I got pretty excited. I have been looking at everyone's hands, and I have seen hands that are funny looking, stubby fingers, long, misshaped fingers, and I've seen beautiful hands. It took me lots of thinking and looking to finally choose someone.

The person's hands I chose are very special to me. She wears a wedding ring on her left hand; they have wrinkles, not many, though. They are little and small for someone her age, but she's small, too. They have held many other hands, given plenty of hugs, touched many shoulders, touched many heads, have held microphones.

Her hands have held many Bibles and flipped through the pages many times. Her hands have taken many others in times of need and encouragement. They have also delivered babies and helped fix people up.

These hands of hers may be small, but they are bigger in many ways than a pair of huge hands. I wish that my hands could be half of what hers may be, to have the hands that many people look for to get support, love, and healing.

These hands I'm talking about belong to my pastor, Angie Cosner.

Rachel

The following poem was given to Pastor Angie by a young man who chose to write of his pain rather than discuss. He explains his pain and his past very poignantly and makes clear the need for programs such as we have on campus and beyond.

A Friend in Pain

There once was a friend of mine
Whose Dad would always beat on him.
Nobody really knew,
And he thought nobody would really care.
But as life went on
He finally got out of that place
He was supposed to call his home.
He lived with his grandparents
For so many years until he had to leave
That place he finally called his home.
Then one day that all ended
And he took a chance on foster care.
Nobody knows how the boy had to live
Except the ones who have felt
That pain each and every day.
They say they know what it was like for the boy
In that home by reading his files.
He knows that's all lies.
He says they will never know
Unless they, too, have felt the pain.
He's lived in three foster homes in the past two years.
Now he's left them and he took a place
In a group home for boys.
He's had trouble
since the day he was born.
People try to help the boy,
But he turns them away
or blocks them out.

Someday he might regret that he's done that—
Someday,
but not today.
He doesn't want them to know
what hell he's gone through
In that home so long ago.
Every day the memories eat him away.
He meets really nice girls, but after a while
He pushes them away and blocks them out.
He doesn't want them to know what he's been through.
He doesn't want his own friends to feel sorry for him, either.
So he goes on with it all inside his mind.
So he tries to live these days like everyone else.
He thinks about those Godforsaken days and wonders,
"Why me? Why does anyone have to go through that pain?"
Because he has never done anything
To that man he calls his dad.
He says, "I was only born. Was that so wrong?"
He asks himself that every day.
He thinks about those days,
But each time he thinks about what happened in those days,
He says, "Maybe it was better that way."
Because he remembers that his brother was safe.
He tries to forget all those bad things in the past.
They always come back from the holes
Where he's buried them in the back of his head.
Right now he's in a new place,
Where nobody knows
what those days have been like
For this fifteen-year-old boy.
He's safe now.
———W.

For My Friend
I thanked God this morning
For giving me a friend like you.
You came along when I needed you the most,
And our friendship did, too.

The special moments we shared
Will be with me forever.
And every day I'll be thankful
That we were brought together.

Thank you for your gift of friendship
And your gift of love.
I wish you all life's best....
Returned to you with love.
Jackie

My Friend...
My friend, I will always be here for you.
My friend, you have been here for me, too.
My friend, we have been through a lot together.
My friendship to you will last forever.
My friend, I will be thinking of you wherever I go.
My friendship will forever be able to flow.
Oneda

Friendship

Friendship is like a doorway,
Or a window to my soul.
The breeze of love flows freely
through
As life struggles take their toll.
I think of you, and I pray for you
Each day as I arise.
'Cause the laughter we share, and the fun we share
Helps the downs of life pass by.

Some Thoughts On Friendship...

Friends are
  Remembered
   In
    Every
     Needed
      Day.
        Jason

Funny...
  Remembering
   In our hearts
    Everywhere we go.
     Near—
      Darn good!
       Mike

Faithful no matter what—
  Reactions we have toward each other...
   Important to one another,
    Even when we fight.
     Never-ending friendship, even when we
      Disagree at times.
        Karissa

Forgiving...
  Reliable...
   Involved in everything I do.
    Exciting...
     Never turning on you.
     Dependable.
     Lisa

"Each friend is a flower…
…in the bouquet of life."
Kathy

Forever being
 Reliable when
  Incidents come up,
   Even when they
    Need to
     Do something else!
      Oneda

Fun…
 Responsible…
  Interesting…
   NEver-ending love…
    Nice…
     Devoted.
      Becky

Forgiving you when you make a mistake.
 Really being true.
  Ignoring your faults.
   Every thing you need them for, they're there to help.
    Never turn their backs on you.
     Do keep secrets.
      Crystal

In the **F**uture
 Remembering the
  Important times,
   Even when you
    Need to
     Discuss things.
      Antonio

> True friends...
> True friends are people you never lose.
> True friends are people you shouldn't abuse.
> True friends are there when you are down.
> True friends are people who never let you frown.
> Lisa

Forget me not...
Remembering me...
Individual...
Everlasting,
Never-ending,
Devotion.
Doug

Forever
Remembering me
In the
Evening,
Noon, and
December light.
Dot

For never taking all the fame,
Right or wrong, always by my side.
Interested in me.
Eager to please.
Never giving up.
Doing with me and beside me.
Katie

Free-spirited and
Ready to cheer
Inside and out...
Even on the worst of days,
Never letting you
Down.
Yolanda

Family

"I'm so glad I'm a part
of the family of God
I've been washed in the fountain
cleansed by His blood!"
Bill Gaither

Family GroupThink

Families are like ice cream on a hot day.

Families are like weeds that grow no matter what.

Families are the snow on the ski slopes of life.

Families are like glass—easily broken.

Families are the busses on the road of life.

A family is a support system that shouldn't let you down.

A family is love that never lasts.

A perfect family is like Big Foot—it doesn't exist.

A family is like an egg—they are fragile and they sometimes stink.

A family is a gift that can't be taken.

Families are like cars—they constantly need repair.

A family is a box that sometimes falls apart.

A family is a pot of gold that never runs out.

When given the opportunity to express themselves, it is not surprising that many of our young people wrote about their mothers. The following piece is typical of what they expressed. Can any one of us read the following and not feel the pain that is expressed and understand the void that is felt in this young person's life? She expresses for all of us our desperate need for love and security.

Mom, where are you?
Please come back.
Don't go any further.
Mom! Mom, I can't see you!
Where are you?
Mom, please don't leave me
with these insane people.
Please, Mom. I love you.
Please don't stop holding me.
Don't stop. Don't stop.
Mom, I am so afraid.
It is so dark.
Mom, I love you
And please don't ever forget....

Mommy,

I am writing to tell you that even though you didn't do quite a good job raising me and my siblings, I forgive you! I miss you more than ever right now. I wish you could see me grow up as your little girl again. I love you with all my heart, but I just need to know one thing: Why?

Love,
Oneda
XOXOXO

Mommy

I forgive you
For everything you have done.
Even though I just
Wanted to hide and run.
You are a special someone
That I love very much
And wish that you could hold me
And your hand I could touch.
I miss you, Mom.
You are the one who had me
And taught me a lot.
Even through the times that we fought.
I wish you were here to see me now
Even though they won't think of it or allow.
You are my mommy, and I wish you were here
To hold me when I shed each tear.

Oneda

*I love you, Mom!
Pumpkin*

My Angel

**You were there when I needed a friend.
You were there to lend me a hand.
You were there to give me all I needed.
You were there to help me succeed.
You were there to give me the best.
You were there to help me rest.
You will always be my angel,
my grandmother.**

Leeann

A Day in My Life at Home

A lonely child sits alone,
No siblings or friend to walk her home.
No laughing or giggling or talking away.
She's just trying to cover her face.
Under that fragile hand is a deep and painful bruise.
That was done by a man drunk on some whiskey and booze.
Some would call him his or her dad.
But would a dad hurt his children this bad?
Where's the mother, everyone seems to ask.
The mother speaks for the dad real fast.
She's convinced that love is there,
But once in a while she'll question where.
She waits on his beckoned call.
She put her life out so he'll never fall.
She loves her children as much as could be.
But still there's a cover over her eyes
So she can't see.
If only more moms could break this chain
Some babies wouldn't have the burden
Of loneliness and endless pain.
But this vicious cycle seems to go on and on
Without a change.

The perpetrators seem to get no shame.
If only the mom would had said stop
The children wouldn't have
Been carried off by a cop.
The children wouldn't be
In an unfamiliar place.
With no one to caress their face.
No one to turn on the little night light.
And, most of all, no one to tell
That they love you,
And no one to say, "I love you, too."
So break the pattern
If it comes along
Before <u>you</u> have children
And <u>you</u> do wrong!
Nikki

A Commitment and A Vow

I had gone away for a while,
And finally my mommy can take us home now.

She made a commitment and a vow
To love and take care of us...
To show us what we need to go through life
And be able to succeed.

So let's go home now, Mom, where we should be
And give all the love you can give to me.
Oneda

If...

If I could feel the pain you do
Then I would help you make your way through.

If I could feel the laughter of happy hearts
Then I would know exactly where to start.

If I could feel the touch of a loving mom
Then I would be safe, secure, and calm.

If I could feel the love of a real dad
Then I wouldn't be sitting here depressed and sad.
Oneda

I Remember

I remember seeing those faces that I once knew
And my mommy saying I was wrong: "It's always you!"
I grabbed my blanket and ran to bed,
Started to cry and covered my head.
I asked myself, "Why me?" and began to hide
All my fears inside.
I became stronger each and every day
Because what I remember is
Living and walking my own way.
Oneda

A little child,
Alone and abused
Ran away from home
With nothing to lose.
Nobody loved her.
Nobody cried.
The little girl
Just died inside.
Her daddy was a sick, sick man.
And worst of all, her mama knew.
But when it came to the fact
Mama said it wasn't true.
Nobody believed the little girl.
What was she to say?
She couldn't wait to grow her wings,
So she could fly away.
As she lay in bed one night
She knew she had to tell.
He had her in a cage
No, it was more like a jail.
The next day the little girl
Confided in a friend.
She told her how she felt
And she wanted it to come to an end.
Now she lives with people who love her.
She's happy, and she's free.
If you believe in this little girl,
Why won't you believe in me?

The Past

Holding on to the past
Not wanting to let go,
I try to think of other things
But the past is all I know.

I try to leave the past behind.
I try to start over again.
But no matter how hard I try
I don't know how to begin.

TL

Child

A child's world falls apart,
Broken bones and a broken heart,
Streaming tears run down his face.
Why was he born to this place?
The unwanted child ran away with a …
Pulled a …….
And now he's gone.

Someday Soon

Someday soon your time will come
To be happy, unlike some.

I would give you the world if I could.
You deserve the best, so someone should.

You've been through a lot over the years,
And you have shed so many tears.

So someday soon it will all come true,
So from now on I'll be praying for you.

                        Oneda

The reason I drew this was because I was thinking of my baby sister, and I miss her. I saw the frog pillow she gave me, so I drew one of the frogs that reminded me what kind of frog Marsha would be. I named this the "Marsha Frog."   Nikki

About Pups and Parting and Past Things...

I am the dog in the window.
I am feeling sad.
My family just left on vacation.
I could not go with them.
Now I am home alone.
I wish I could have gone.
I wish I had someone to play with……
     Elizabeth

"I think and wonder if I should go home."

The puppy misses his mom. He is really sad.
His mom just went to the vet, and he
doesn't have anyone to play with…
    Kristal

I'm wondering what exists out there
further than the window sill.
Curious, but not troublesome.
Relaxed.
Freeminded.
Lonesome for a friend, but not worried.
     Nikki

45

Will my brothers and sisters be all gone soon?
Will my mom be sold, too?
Will I be the only one left?
Will they remember me?
Will I remember them?
What will it be like without them?
Will I ever see them again?
Why?

Where are they taking him? I thought I was his best friend. He was supposed to be there until the end. Now who will take care of me? Who will set me free? I'm locked in this house. I feel trapped. I am in need. You were my best friend, don't you see?
Leeann

Why Weren't You There?
Why weren't you here the day I left
To say that I was someone you truly accept?

Why weren't you here to say that you love me
To be by my side and tell me that we were meant to be?

Why weren't you here to show me that you care?
Why weren't you? It would only be fair.
Oneda

Feelings

"Our feelings are
our most genuine paths
to knowledge."
Audre Lorde

 # Feelings GroupThink

Love is the sun to all living things.

Anger is like an open space that will never give shelter.

Fear is a monster that attacks us all.

Love is a potion that everybody deserves.

Anger is like a bomb that will eventually blow up.

Anger is a knot in your rope that is hard to get out.

Love is a language that speaks to all people.

Emotions are a bunch of balloons that sometimes pop.

Emotions are bottled up like a genie in a bottle.

Anger is a volcano that will sometimes erupt.

Love is the main ingredient in the cook book of life.

Emotions are a crayon box that has all different kinds.

Emotions are confusion that soon will be revealed.

Happiness

To find the meaning of happiness, our first thought would be to look up the word in the dictionary. But happiness cannot be described in just a few words. I think each and every person defines happiness in a different way.

I believe it comes from within our mind, body, and soul.

We might say happiness is a cool breeze on a hot summer day...

...or a polite "Excuse me" when someone stands in your way....

...a smile from a friend across a crowded room...

...a handshake of a stranger that you never knew...

...a gentle touch of a baby's hand...

...a hard day's labor and...

...well-earned pay...

...our friends around noisily having fun..

...reading a book all alone in an empty room...

...our family and our friends....

Anything in life that is good and promotes goodness can be defined as happiness.

Happiness needs to be shared.

We could say if money is the root of all evil, then God must be the root of all happiness.

The only place you can find happiness before love is in the dictionary.

Mike

Feeling Happy……...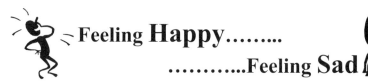
………..Feeling Sad

"I feel happy when I'm dancing in the middle of the living room with my brother and sister. I don't have a care in the world. We dance so much that we collapse in a pile on the couch. I always tell them how much I love them. I feel happy just being there and holding them. They are almost my whole life."
TL

"I feel happy when I swim in the sea.
I feel free and know Jesus is near me."
Chris

"I feel happy when I am hangin' out with my friends. It gives me time to unwind and talk about anything that's on my mind. It gives me a chance to be myself and to have fun without worrying about what anyone thinks or getting into trouble."
Marco

"I feel sad when the sky is gray... I feel sad when my world is crushed and swept away to forever be forgotten. I feel sad when a puppy dies, and there is nothing I can do to bring it back. I feel sad when the rain falls heavy, and the flood waters rise to the point of extinction……...I feel sad forever."
Roy

"I feel sad when I'm played around with or hurt…....when someone talks about my family."
Crystal

Feeling Happy……..
…………..Feeling Sad

"I feel sad when I think about all these kids that say they have nothing when they have everything they need. Now think about the kids who <u>really</u> don't have anything. It really makes me sad."
Leann

"I feel sad when I follow my peers, and I get let down or used….when someone hurts my feelings…..I'm not wanted by anyone….when my self-esteem or self worth is very low…..when my family disowns me….when I get into a fight or argument."
Oneda

The things that make me happy are:

- ☺ being with my family
- ☺ being able to help people
- ☺ playing basketball and soccer
- ☺ pumpkin pie and spaghetti
- ☺ being in my warm bed
- ☺ when I get praised or complimented
- ☺ being with my dog Angel
- ☺ when people don't argue
- ☺ looking at my pictures
- ☺ having good memories
- ☺ when I see someone accept the Lord and I can witness to them

Oneda

Who I am is delicate and fragile....so much so, at times I am untouchable. And yet the touching is what I yearn for the most. Without it I suffer endless grief....I am abandoned and alone. Rejection is the place where I go and there is where I live out my pain.

A seed has the audacity to believe it can grow. It will push out of itself and find direction. It will know its purpose and ignore the flood and the drought. It will push beyond its own limits through elements immeasurably stronger than itself. And it will survive!

Survive. Weather. Endure. To burst open with exquisite elation. To stand tall in the heat of the day. To graciously bow in the wind and make the storm its dance. To live.

Who I am is delicate and fragile....so much so, at times I am untouchable. But it isn't the flower's fault if no one stops to smell it.

It blooms anyway.

Linda

Looking at the World from a Different Viewpoint

I am that one special toy that was given to you as a young child. We did everything together. We celebrated birthdays, Christmases, Easters, and many other holidays together. Even though I couldn't open my lips to say how much I love you, you knew. My best friend was a little girl named Nikki and your best friend was a little china doll you got for your eighth birthday from your momma.

Remember, you called me Sarah? I was so sure that I would never feel the darkness of a box cover or dust collecting over my china doll face. Years have gone by, and so have many changes. I no longer sit on the high throne——the highest pillow on your small bed. I now have cracks in my porcelain hands and my paint is slowly deteriorating with time. Memories are the number one thing that keep me in any kind of high spirits that you will reach on that high shelf in your closet and pull down that box and pull me out and hug me as though you were eight again, not eighteen. But until

then, the memories will keep me going. I have no choice but to sit in the emptiness of my long, rectangle box that you took me out of so long ago, but put me back into so recently.

Nikki

My Cloak

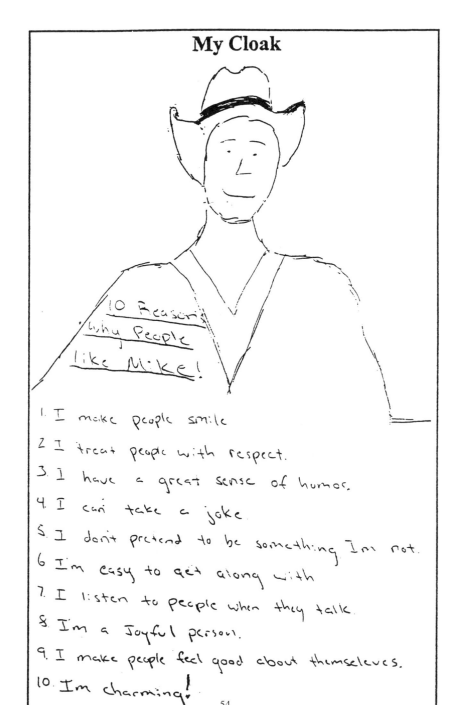

10 Reasons Why People like Mike!

1. I make people smile
2. I treat people with respect.
3. I have a great sense of humor.
4. I can take a joke
5. I don't pretend to be something I'm not.
6. I'm easy to get along with
7. I listen to people when they talk.
8. I'm a Joyful person.
9. I make people feel good about themseleves.
10. I'm charming!

My Cloak

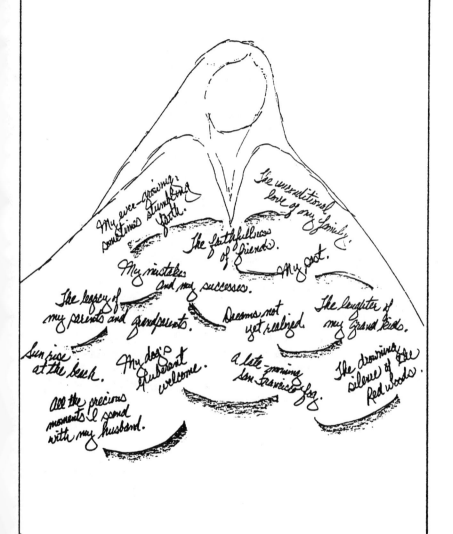

My Cloak

I love to achieve and not receive, because I love to work at stuff so I make myself stronger mentally.

So take life as it comes. Love yourself, and you will achieve more goals. So love yourself and others.

My Cloak

My cloak is a valuable thing that I keep in my heart at all times.

These things are all very special to me!
-Oneda-

Asking individuals to respond to this year in their life can be surprising and insightful. In his very short response, this young man reveals much about himself. It serves as a reminder that during our lives, we deal with many obstacles and hardships ——some far more than others. And yet, despite the trials and frustrations, many of us—especially our youth——are able to maintain a positive outlook about the future. Perhaps that's what learning and growing and believing is all about.

Nineteen

A year of friends and family dying and thinking about suicide,
but the Lord stopped me.
I'm looking forward to getting out on my own.
I'm excited about going to Heaven and seeing my dad.
I'm nervous about life.
And I fear that I will not make it to Heaven.
All in all, life can be a big dream
we have not wakened up from yet.

Art

At This Time in My Life.......

Seventeen
A year of pain and frustration.
I'm looking forward to college.
I'm excited about being a senior.
I'm nervous about letting myself down.
And I fear failure.
All in all, life can be frustrating.
Chris

Seventeen
A year of frustration and fun.
I'm looking forward to finishing school.
I'm excited about going home.
I'm nervous about the future.
And I fear water.
All in all, life can be a long road.
Mike

Seventeen
A year of love and pain.
I'm looking forward to being someone powerful.
I'm excited about being with someone special.
I'm nervous about the future.
And I fear being institutionalized.
All in all, life is good and bad.
Antonio

Seventeen

A year of excitement and nervousness.
I'm looking forward to being an adult.
I'm excited about turning eighteen.
I'm nervous about turning eighteen.
And I fear turning eighteen.
All in all, life is very difficult to approach.
Marco

Seventeen

A year of confusion and changes.
I'm looking forward to going home for good.
I'm excited about turning eighteen.
I'm nervous about whether or not
I'll be able to make it.
And I fear that I will fail in life.
All in all, life is scary but rewarding.
Nikki

Seventeen and a Half

A year of odds and evens.
I'm looking forward to going home.
I'm excited about being eighteen.
I'm nervous about my eighteenth birthday.
And I fear death.
All in all, life can be fun and sad.
Jason

Sixteen
A year of growing and learning.
I'm looking forward to better relationships.
I'm excited about independence.
I'm nervous about following my boundaries.
And I fear dying in water.
All in all, life is a fine balance.
Teresa

Sixteen
A year of fear and confusion.
I'm looking forward to being loved
by the one I love.
I'm excited about things
I have accomplished in life.
I'm nervous about not being good enough.
And I fear losing what I have.
All in all, life is hard to deal with
And get what you need done, done.
Crystal

Sixteen
A year of worries and hurt.
I'm looking forward to being on my own.
I'm excited about being with the one I love.
I'm nervous about being on my own.
And I fear going back home.
All in all, life is full of obstacles.
Lisa

Sixteen
A year of laughter and having fun.
I'm looking forward to getting out on my own.
I'm excited abut being with my boyfriend.
I'm nervous about what's going to happen between us.
And I fear that it's not gonna work.
All in all, life can be great.
Karissa

Fifteen
A year of happiness and frowns.
I'm looking forward to going back home.
I'm excited about being myself.
I'm nervous about messing up at home again.
And I fear going home.
All in all, life can be pretty good.
Tim

Fifteen
A year of peace and hope.
I'm looking forward to going home.
I'm excited about seeing my mom.
I'm nervous about starting school.
And I fear people not liking me.
All in all, life is what you make it.
Liz

Fifteen
A year of worries and confusion.
I'm looking forward to going home in three years.
I'm excited about being loved when I am home.
I'm nervous about meeting new people.
And I fear losing someone close to me.
All in all, life can be a very painful but joyful situation.
Leeann

Fourteen
A year of rejection and peer pressure.
I'm looking forward to being older.
I'm excited about being in tenth grade.
I'm nervous about making new friends.
And I fear not fitting in.
All in all, life is emotional and exciting.
Oneda

Thirteen
A year of fun and games.
I'm looking forward to going places.
I'm excited about Apple Harvest.
I'm nervous about new places.
And I fear the devil.
All in all, life is like sand.
Kristal

Thirteen
A year of being responsible and having responsibility.
I'm looking forward to living my life, not theirs.
I'm excited about being free.
I'm nervous about going out into the world.
And I fear nothing.
All in all, life is just another brick in the wall.
Marcus

During the meetings of our creative arts classes, our campus staff participate in the activities along with the residents. The following are some interesting responses about periods in their lives—past or present—as they reflected with the youth during the activity. Their participation serves as role models for the youth and their support is always greatly appreciated!

Fifty-one

A year of good feelings and stress.
I'm looking forward to getting away.
I'm excited about my peace of mind.
I'm nervous about my son.
And I fear losing my youth.
All in all, life is good.

Doug

Fifty

A year of grandchildren and memories.
I'm looking forward to joyful times.
I'm excited about becoming a new grandmother.
I'm nervous about their future.
And I fear the unknown.
All in all, life is heaven sent.

Katie

Twenty-five

A year of physical pain and excitement.
I'm looking forward to holding my child.
I'm excited about what I am having.
I'm nervous about being a mother.
And I fear labor.
All in all, life can be a stressful but a fulfilling adventure.

Melinda

Twenty-three

A year of bittersweet changes.
I'm looking forward to the birth of my first child.
I'm excited about having a family.
I'm nervous about knowing everything
a mom should know.
And I fear I might miss my independence.
All in all, life is excitingly full of awesome wonder.

Linda

Walking into a residential unit or observing the interaction on campus, one can see and feel the love of the staff for the youth they serve. A sense of family——with all the hugs and joys and trials and struggles—is evident. The bonding of hearts and souls can not be denied. The following is a touching explanation of the calling felt by many staff members who serve our campus, for it is truly a calling and a ministry——much more than a job——to those who give and love and nurture our youth as they struggle to understand their lives and seek their place in the world.

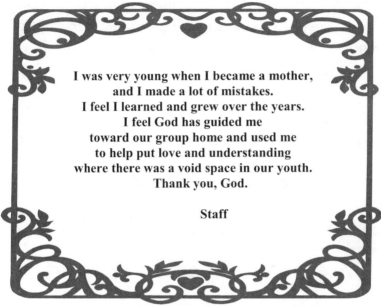

I was very young when I became a mother,
and I made a lot of mistakes.
I feel I learned and grew over the years.
I feel God has guided me
toward our group home and used me
to help put love and understanding
where there was a void space in our youth.
Thank you, God.

Staff

From the Kitchen of Shirl and Katie...

Childcare's Lifetime Recipe
2 heaping cups of patience
1 heart full of love
2 handfuls of generosity
Dash of laughter
1 head full of understanding

 **Just thinking to myself…..**

I've always wanted to commit myself to being Christ-like. I can see myself someday being a missionary when I pull myself together again. That's very important to me.

If I could give anyone the best advice I could, it would be to be yourself, stand strong, and keep your head up through thick and thin.

Make the best out of what you do have!

Love yourself before learning to love others.

The way you think is how you feel.

You are a gift from God!
Oneda

 # Looking Backward, Moving Forward

Looking back at what home used to be
I remember what it was like for me.

Coming home from school on a hot day
Wondering what to do or say.

Looking back to all of this
Isn't what I wanted to see
Because I remember
What it used to be.
                Karissa

She's looking at the farmhouse and crying in the field she used to play in. The old run down farmhouse is caving in. It's not what it used to be.

    Crystal

Looking back at this old farmhouse
Makes me want to cry
Because the years as a little girl
Just flew by.

A little girl looking back at her home,
Remembering how it used to be.

And when I look at the old house
While sitting in the tall grass,
I'm saying this to myself,
"This isn't what I wanted to see."

It used to be a time
Of happiness and love.
But now it's lonely
With no one around.
I wonder if the presence of them is surrounding this place.

Time to go home now.
Things will never be the same.
But I am glad I came!
Oneda

Hiding from her parents,
They are fighting again,
Wishing she could run away
And leave this world of sin.
If only she were older,
She could find a place to turn.
If only ……………..
She would………..
Teresa

Looking at the picture…..I think about when I was a little girl, sitting in the grass, looking at the house, and thinking about what is going on——being afraid to go back to the house because of mom and dad's fighting.
Becky

About **Struggles** and **Goals** and **Life**...

These are taken from lines of poetry, reaction to writing prompts, or from discussions within our group. Regardless of the source, the thoughts of the young people as they reveal themselves to us show wisdom and insight far beyond their years.

"Broken hearts may never heal completely. For when the next time they want somebody, they'll remember the last."
TL

"Losing everything that means the most to you is like giving everyone else up, too."

"All I need in life to feel good is God."
Elizabeth

"Take my hand and I will make you see. Give me the chance that I need to get through life, so that I can succeed."
OD

"Deep in my heart, it screams *love.*
　　Deep in my mind, it screams *hate.*"

Why was it me, an innocent child, hurt by someone I dearly love? I did nothing wrong, yet I was hurt for so very long. You shattered my heart and battered my soul. Why was it my life that was torn apart? But now that you have chains holding you back, my feelings, thoughts, and hate I can share.
LM

More About **Struggles** and **Goals** and **Life...** **.....And Love**

"Love is like a ride at the amusement park...you can't wait to get on, but you feel sick when they put you off."
                              Teresa

"Life is special, but precious. It can end as fast as it began. You're born—you die. And in between you do whatever you please. Even though your heart says "no," your mind says "go." You live so fast, your life passes you by. And then you stop and look around and you realize you have no one but yourself. All through life, you thought friendship was nothing. But then at that moment, you realize there's only one true friend. And that's the friend in yourself. And you need no one else."   Crystal

"I need to love myself for who I really am, not for others but for me because myself is what I want and need to be."
                              Oneda

"God has a funny way of telling us down here that life has something special in store for us. I truly believe that the ones such as myself who have had the hardcore life will survive with a gold medal. But then again, there are some victims who stay victims for the rest of their lives. Why? Because they have no reassurance that life will get better. I do have that reassurance. I gave it to myself the day that I decided that when I grew up, I was gonna be a social worker. How could I go into an occupation such as this and be a complete walking bomb, ready to explode at any given moment? I had to be strong for all the kids that my attitude and emotions affect."
                              Nikki

My Code of Honor

1. Put God before anything else.
2. Be there for my family and friends at all times.
3. Treat others as I would like to be treated ——respectfully……
4. Never underestimate what the Lord can and will do.
5. Honor the Father up above.
6. Never judge someone.
7. Feel good about who you are.
8. Be thankful for what you <u>do</u> have.
9. Don't put anyone in a situation that you wouldn't want to be in.
10. Take care of your body and love yourself……

Oneda

"Love, above everything, is the gift to one's self."

Some food for thought…..

+The road to Heaven is paved with joy, faith, and hard work.
+An object that is important to me would be my Bible because it holds the word of God.
+My greatest talent would be my manners. I use them often. I use them to be kind to others.

Elizabeth

The Warm Feeling

It's like a warm breeze—
or the sun coming over a hill.
It makes a smile come to me—
That's how love makes me feel.

My eyes have a glow—
Nothing can bring me down.
My happiness shows—
Whenever he comes around.

We laugh, play, and cuddle—
Each day brings more love.
Whether away or close enough to snuggle,
He's the one I think of.

Elizabeth

Beneath All of This

Beneath all of this body
I have feelings that one can't see.
They are real and sometimes painful.
Beneath all this, there is a real me.
Someplace out there
I will begin to see
What life was made to be.
Beneath all this,
there is someone special
Who is loved for what she *is* and *can be*.

Oneda

Ugly Things

big ears
dead eyes
buck teeth
large thighs
wide feet
long nose
flat chest
ugly toes
bum knees
enormous butt
breaking nails
fat gut
birth marks
sun spots
puffy hair
acne dots

These may be ugly things,
But in the end
God gives us wings.
TL

When the Tears Start To Fall

When the tears start to fall
And the hurt begins to build up inside
It hurts because you feel there is no place to hide.
Please give me something to fill up my emptiness
So I can get over all my loneliness.
Give me a tissue to wipe up my tears
And wrap your arms around me
To take away all my fears.

Oneda

Please Don't Judge Me

Please don't judge me
by what you see,
Instead please look inside of me.
Please don't judge me
by my color or race
Because I wouldn't want anyone
to take my place.
Please don't judge me
for all the bad things I do
Because I know I am not perfect,
And neither are you.
Oneda

Things I Love

I love the quiet,
When nobody speaks,
When the birds don't chirp
And the mice don't squeak.

I love the dark,
When there's no light,
When you don't see a soul
Anywhere in sight.

I love being alone,
All by myself,
Like a doll in the closet,
In a box, on the top shelf.
TL

Father's Disguise
cuts on my arms
bruises on my legs
cuts on my back
bruises on my face

scared to breathe
afraid to talk
scared to look
afraid to walk

wanting to leave
needing to go
wanting to tell
needing to show

run away
hide from the eyes
run to a safe place
leave his disguise

TL

I am...
I am a lost bird who has a broken wing.
I am locked in a cage and would like to sing.

I am a dead tree whose leaves have fallen off.
I am someone who would like to laugh.

I am a little girl who is trying to find the way.
I am an old woman who has nothing to say....

I am watching the angels dancing around.
I am listening to Jesus without making a sound.

I am finally happy.......to know who I am.
Oneda

Help

Help me, for I am still young.
I need a shoulder to lean on.
**Get away, for I am a teenager
and can make my own decision.**
Help me, for I am confused. I am a teenager.
But I have some kid in me that wants to stay.
I have never gotten to play.
**Get away, for I don't need help.
With help comes closeness, then friendship.**
Help me, for I am lost.
I have no one.
I pushed everyone away
Because of my anger and hatred toward
the world.
All I want is love.
Can you help me?
     Crystal

They are my world
They won my heart when they were born.
When I saw them unhappy or sad, it tore me apart
And broke my heart.
When I had to raise them
It took my childhood away,
But I ♥ every minute of it.
Because they are my life.
They made me work for what I have now
And look forward to life
For they are part of my soul.
They are the goal to my heart.
When we got separated the first time
It hurt me a lot.
Now that we get to see each other
It won't be the same again,
But I ♥ them until the end.

     Crystal

Doors—
Opportunities or Barriers?

"I can see out through the crack in the door. It gives me hope of a good day."
    Jay

"I'm going to go outside to see the world around me, no hurt or pain for once. The water is blue and sparkly as September diamonds. The trees are as full as fall. And through it all someone out there is waiting on me that loves me for me."
    Crystal

"When I became a resident of Burlington, I decided to shut and lock the door to my past and open the door to my future."
    Teresa

"Going out a door to a new life by giving your life to God. He is the one you give your heart to."
    A.T.

"I am inside my home about to go outside to the back of my wonderful backyard where my beautiful flowers and big pool is, so I can relax and get stuff off my mind. I go back to my yard to enjoy the feeling of being happy. I love the feeling of being happy."
    Karissa

"I could be opening a door to a whole new world of love, peace, and happiness. It reminds me of a part of my life when I was unhappy and someone opened a door for me that brought me to be a whole new person. Realizing that if you want happiness in your life, you have to be willing to open the door and take a chance. Don't close it and lose what could have been!"   Melinda

 "I am opening the door, getting ready to go into the world which I have been isolated from."
                Lisa

"Why am I here? Do I hide all my fear?"
            Leeann

 "As I open the door to see who's been knocking, I feel a gentle breeze. When the door is open, I realize it is my sister, who has come to visit me. I welcome her and invite her in to catch up on our past."
                            Elizabeth

"A man is opening the door, and only he knows where he is going."   Mike

 "The person is me opening the door to go check on my rabbit. When I did, at the doorstep is a stray pup."
                    Kristal

"I see a man or woman opening a door to a new world, or it could be Heaven."   Art

78

> A knob to close
> A key to lock.
> When someone needs you,
> They will knock.
> A peephole to see
> Who's coming your way,
> Someone to greet you,
> Or make your day.
> Oneda

"For my short time at Burlington, I am at the boys' group home. The group home is where all the boys work through their problems by talking things out to keep the group home's name good in Keyser. The reason I am in state's custody is because my grandmother died. This time in Burlington is my door of opportunity to better myself day to day, so when I am eighteen to take life as it comes. In reality, the door of Burlington opens your future to life in a new beginning. Take the time to learn all new things. These are my words of truth and experience. So take life as it comes, take heed, and learn from yourself."

Jason

> I shut the door on life sometimes
> when the outside world gets too big
> or scary
> or too difficult to handle.
> Once the door is closed, I feel safe
> and calm
> and ALONE
> and that's okay——<u>for a while.</u>
> Linda

"Someone is turning the knob to go outside. They go bag the pile of leaves up in their front yard. Then they tell the kids to come in for dinner."   Tim

"I see a woman coming home from work. It is dusk, and the woman is closing the door for the night."

Marco

"Leaving here is really scary. I don't know what's out there, and I am scared but excited. If only my mom would have been here, I wouldn't have to do this on my own. But I'm alone. I mean, I'm not physically alone, but deep down inside, I'm alone.

What's out there? Will I have enough strength to make it on my own?

Help!! I can't do this! Someone help!

Sure, I can do this. Whether or not I want to do this, I have to. It's a matter of survival. I have to prove that I can and will survive. I've got the strength. Ready or not, I'm ready to chance my life on it."
Nikki

Dreams
They seem so true.
They seem so meaningful.
But all they are,
Are lost hopes in the wind
Just waiting to be caught.
They eventually just fade with the sunlight.
To every lost dream out there,
they belong to a lost soul,
Someone who wanted it so badly
But never got a chance to experience it.
And when it doesn't come soon enough,
You lose that hope that dreams require
And it just fades away without any traces behind.
Not even memories.
Because you never got to experience
Those feelings of happiness that you get
From knowing you did something
That you did.
Nikki

I See It All...

I am a blanket that Oneda keeps on her bed. I know I am important to her because I keep her warm, and she comes to me when she cries. She has had me for fourteen years, and I look kind of old—a hole at the bottom. I remember when she got me. It was her first Christmas. When I felt her pick me up, I remember thinking, "How are you going to treat me? Will you love me?" Because I was wanting a home and someone to take care of me. I am happy that I am with Oneda because I've been treated well and cared for. My time with her has turned out to be wonderful and enjoyable. I've seen her cry, and I always know how she is feeling."

Note: (My blanket is very special to me because when I am upset, I cover up with it. When I was little, I would wrap all in it, and I put a hole in the bottom because of my feet.)

I am a picture that Jason keeps near his bed. I know I am important to him because I am always in his mind. He has had me for two years, and I look brand new. I remember when they got me. It was the day he was born on November 7, 1983. When I saw them pick me up, I remember thinking that I am the truth in his life. I am happy that I am with Jason.

"Our memories are our window to the past and part of our journey to the future."

 I am the picture that Crystal keeps above the head of the bed. I know I am important to her because I am a picture of her mom. She has had me for two years, and I look in good shape. I remember when she got me. It was from her cousin Anita. When I felt her pick me up, I remember thinking how she had grown and was happy. She was so big and so happy when she got me. I am happy that I am with Crystal because she kisses me every night and tells me she loves me. My time with her has turned out to be wonderful and happy because she loves me.

I am a teddy bear that Becky keeps on her bed. I know I am important to her because her sister gave me to her. She has had me for two months, and I look as good as a button. I remember when she got me. I was a birthday present that her sister got for her. When I felt her pick me up, I remember thinking that she  was going to love me and keep me forever because her sister gave me to her and she will cherish me for life. I am happy that I am with Becky because she treats me good. My time with her has turned out to be good.

 I am a watch that Mike keeps on his wrist. I know I am important to him because I keep him on time. He has had me for yearssssss, and I look new. When he got me, it was no special occasion. When he picked me up, I remember thinking, "You're late!" because he didn't have a watch. I am happy that I am with Mike because he's treated me good. My time with him has been great because he's on time now.

I am a scooter that Chris keeps downstairs. I know I am important to him because his brother gave me to him. He has had me for a year, and I look new. I remember when he got me. I was a gift from his brother. When he picked me up, I remember thinking that he was so excited because I was once his brother's. I am happy that I am with Chris because he takes good care of me. My time with him has turned out to be good because I know he enjoys me.

I am a bear that Marco keeps in his closet. I know I am important to him because I was there for him through everything. He has had me for thirteen years, and I look worn and torn. I remember when he got me. It was at a yard sale, and I was nothing special. When he picked me up, I remember thinking that he was really happy , and I was sure I had a home for life. He wouldn't put me down. I am happy that I am with Marco because he has treated me well.

I am a heart full of love that Lisa keeps with hers——I am her grandmother's love. She has had me for seventeen years and I am the same as always. I remember the day Lisa was born. When she let me in (her heart), I remember thinking, "She looks happy." I knew she felt loved. I am happy that I am still with Lisa because she has loved me from the start. My time with her has turned out to be warm and full of love.

*"When I look into their eyes,
I can see their hearts."
Pastor Angie*

I am a book that Dot keeps on her nightstand. She has had me for a long time, and I still look new but worn. I was a special gift from a friend. When I felt her pick me up, I remember thinking how surprised and happy I was to be with Dot because she is gentle with me. My time with her has been special.

I am a dog that Doug keeps in his house. I know I am important to him because he's happy and content when I am around. He has had me for twelve years, and I look old. I remember when he got me. I was a gift for him, and I cost $25.00. I remember him taking me to bed with him the first night and still does today. I was happy and excited. I am happy that I am with Doug because he treats me the best every day I am with him. My time with him has turned out to be comfortable and relaxing. We always look forward to seeing one another.

I am a chain that Chris keeps around his neck. I know I am important to him because he wears it all the time. He has had me for three days, and I look new. I remember when he got me. It was something that he picked out to buy. When he picked me up, I remember thinking, "That looks hot," because I was wanting to be worn by someone cool. I am happy to be with Chris. My life with him has turned out to be a never-ending story.

"I am a wedding band that Teresa keeps on her right ring finger. I know I am important to her because I hold a lot of memories of her grandmother. She has had me for a little over a year, and I look the same as when her grandmother owned me. I remember when she got me. It was right after her grandmother's funeral. When she picked me up, I remember thinking that this event must be very hard for her because she was crying while holding me in her palm. I am proud that I am with Teresa because I have been with her through a big change. My time with her has turned out to be very eventful and full of sorrow."

Prejudice for the World

Who do you hate?
Do you think it's right,
To hate someone
Because your black
And they're white?
Or because you're smart,
And they're not so bright?
Everyone's different.
Nothing's new.
I'm sorry if nobody's
The same as you.
We're all different,
But we're all the same.
You're different to me,
So who's to blame?
Roy

Only You

My life is breaking down.
Your voice is breaking up.
Every time I talk to you
I never want to hang it up.
I can smell you on my pillow.
You're always on my mind.
All the ways you touch me
Send chills up and down my spine.
The only thing I want is to
Hear you on the phone.
I always knew I'd love you.
I'll never leave you alone.
I'm staring out my window.
Hoping to see you.
I've been standing here since 12.
Now it's 2:02.
Then I finally realize it's past 4:15,
And to really live is just sufferinggggggg.
Only you can bring me down
The way you doooooooo…..
Roy

Some Thoughts About Campus…..

"I think Burlington is compared to like a Holiday Inn because we have more freedom than other places. Some of the other hospitals have lock down. You only get one hour outside. Here you can go outside any time you want, but staff has to know where you are. I suggest that whoever needs help should come to Burlington."

And Some Clever Comparisons About *Staff* and *Campus*

Burlington is like an Advil—— they're always taking the pain away.

"Burlington is like a garage that fixes broken things."

"Burlington is like a napkin—— they're always there to catch the spill."

"Burlington is like a harbor that provides rest for its travelers."

"Burlington is like good sportsmanship— it doesn't matter whether you are a winner or a loser."

"Burlington is like a rock—— they're always standing strong for their kids."

**Life without kids?
——Unimaginable!
A.T.**

"I see a girl that has been walking through a field of grass. She has made a wreath out of some of the grass she has picked from the winding path. This path is kind of like life——it has many twists and turns in it."

Marco

She walks around,
She thinks it's without a cause.
But deep down inside she knows
     Everything has its flaws.
She goes that way and this....
     She says to herself,
"If I only had one wish...."

Lisa

**What should I say?
I was being nice.
Now should I follow the path she has taken,
Or go my own way?
Maybe all she needs is time,
The anger will go away,
And she will come back and play.
John**

"Lingering in a field, wanting to be lost——far from home. Suddenly she realizes that she misses her family and picks flowers for them. She takes one last look before heading home."

Crystal

"I was walking through the wheat field on my farm, thinking of how my life could be better and how I felt so alone. My grandfather had died, and he cared very much about his farm. I decided I wanted to take a wreath of flowers to his grave. All of a sudden, I heard a cry. It was my brother yelling, "If you wanna go to his grave, Dad is leavin' now." I said, "Hold on." I looked up at the sky and asked, "Why can't you be here with me?"

Valleri

       I like him…he is sweet.
       He follows me around the place
       Like a baby to its mamma.

       He does not talk..
              He does not speak
       For his eyes tell it all.
          They tell he's shy….he hides thoughts
…….that are ingenious to the world….
these he knows he holds……..
….but is scared to let them go.

       Maybe his voice will tell me someday
       Of his thoughts he hides away.
For he is like a candle wanting to burn……
Burn brighter than all the rest.
              Cassie

I'm all alone……….
       No one to talk to.
    Oh, why can't they understand me?
    I'm in love with a boy who is in love with me,
    But my mom does not approve of me
     being with him.
    What shall I do?
    My love for him is so deep.
    I was to meet him an hour ago.
    He's late again. Oh, well….
    I'll give him five more minutes..
    Wait, here he comes!
       What do I do?
          I love him so much.
             What do I do?
                Leeann

Blessings

Bless the moon, bless the sky, bless the light,
bless the good, bless the bad, bless the happy,
bless the sad, bless the poor, bless the rich,
bless the wrong, bless the right, bless the boy,
bless the girl, bless the water, bless the sea.
After you have blessed all that,
Please, Lord, bless me!
Leeann

"An object that is important to me is my blanket that I had gotten on my first Christmas. My mom used to tell me that I would wrap all in it, suck on my bottle, and have my feet in the little pocket at the bottom. That blanket means a lot to me. It brings back a lot of memories."
Oneda

"What I value most in life is a black and white checkered baby blanket. When I was little, I stole it from my brother, but he knew how much I wanted it, so he gave it to me. I won't let anyone steal it.

I have this pillow that my dad gave me when I was little. I have had that pillow for four years. I sleep with it every night."
Kristal

A quote to represent my life would be this:
"A child feeling she's all alone in this world
wondering what to do or where to turn,
looking to God and letting Him
help me deal with my concerns."
Oneda

Christmas Thoughts, Christmas Memories

Christmas is the birth of Jesus. Christmas is when family members get together to exchange gifts, eat a big dinner, tell stories——just a time to be together.
     Elizabeth

"Christmas is a new birth and a new beginning for all of us."
     Karissa

Christmas is a time to recognize our place in the world—recognize who brought you here, and who you're actually celebrating. Christmas is a holiday which has been blown out of proportion. People no longer believe in the true meaning.
     Nikki

Christmas is.....

Christmas is a starving homeless man sitting on an alleyway and somebody brings him pumpkin pie.

Christmas is a little child in hiding....bruises and cuts over his body and on his face—and a kind person wipes his eyes.

Christmas is a stray dog wandering into a neighborhood and finding a family who will take him in.

Christmas is a time I was with my family, but that will never happen again.
     TL

Christmas is a day of thanks, happiness, joy, love, peace, trust, faith, and enjoying the Christmas get-together with your families. Christmas is the time to celebrate Jesus's birthday and to pray for those who need help, who are sick and have problems. Christmas is a time to sit and relax and praise the Lord—to make every day a good one because things can come so quickly.

                Tanganika

Christmas is a time for love and joy,
the smiles spread across a child's face when they receive a toy.

Christmas is far-fetched from what other people say,
but Christmas was a very special day.

When Jesus was born, it spread throughout the earth
because on December 25 was the day of his birth.

So when you think of Christmas always remember
it's a time of giving, loving, joy, celebration,
and the beginning of a new life.
                Oneda

"Hanukah is a ten day holiday where you get a different gift each day. It's a time where families get together."
                Becky

Christmas means to me when Jesus was born. Nowadays we put up a tree. We give each other presents. Christmas is when God chose a gift for the baby Jesus. That was the North Star.
                Kristal

What Christmas Means to Me

As young children, we are raised with the belief that Christmas is a time for getting presents, eating lots of candy, and spending time with your family, but mostly playing with the new toys. Most children even know the story of how Christmas came to be and why it's important to share.

As we grow up, we find that it's not just the joy brought about by the gifts, but the feelings we get inside when we give them. Then the true spirit of Christmas comes into the light—sharing the joys of life and love with one another. Spending money to buy gifts and preparing the traditional dinner are just methods to bring the family together so they can spend time with one another. It's one of those times of the year to decorate and spread joy all over. Even during the decorating of the house and the tree, families take the time to be closer to each other, and to me, that is what makes Christmas an enjoyable experience. Even though you can't always spend that time with the ones you love most, it is a great time wherever you are and whomever you are with.

Jay

A Christmas Memory

Waking up to a morning full of surprises, wondering what Santa was to bring. Hearing carolers outside my windows as they begin to sing. Running out to wake my mom to gather around the tree; opening presents one by one to see what Santa had brought to me. Shouting with laughter and joy while I hold my hand full of toys. The Christmas lights are all shining bright, and my dad is nowhere in sight. I run to my mom and put my arms around her neck and ask, "What did you expect?"

Oneda

Future

"Never be afraid
to trust an unknown future
to a known God."
Corrie Ten Boom

Future GroupThink

Goals are dreams that lead to happiness.

Growing up is a journey that has many winding paths.

Memories are everlasting photos.

Life is a book that needs to be read.

Goals are like dreams that might come true.

Goals are like opportunities that need to be fulfilled.

Growing up is a h_ _ _ that is torturous to us all.

Goals are like a game that you strive to win.

Memories are unending feelings that continue like a rainstorm.

Memories are our ties to the past and our link to the future.

Growing up is a journey that has an indefinite end.

Growing up is like a marathon where not everyone is in shape.

Goals are like shoes—you need new ones and they have to fit.

Me

One day I'll be free.
One day I'll be able to see
What I want to be….

…….be in life….
...survive the
Unsurvivable pain
I have inside of me.

This pain and confusion
I feel sometimes is unbearable.
And a special person comes along
And helps me
Float my troubles and pain
Out to sea.

I watch the pains and troubles float away,
And I want to grab them and bring them back
For I have become attached to them.
That special person
I found out all along I had with me
Was me.
So I can do it!
One day I'll be free
One day I'll be able to see
What I want to be.
And know what it is——
Me.

Crystal

Ten Years From Now…..

"Ten years from now, I imagine myself being a social worker and being a mom with two beautiful kids and having my own house."

"Ten years from now, I can imagine myself with a big family and with a big house, hoping to hurry up and retire."
Mike

"Ten years from now, I can imagine myself being a psychologist—a psychologist helping families and kids stay together…."
Becky

"Ten years from now, I can imagine myself in college with a good job."
Crystal

"Ten years from now, I want to be in college….I want to be a criminologist. I want to be with someone who really cares for me, for who I am. I want to make my life worth something. I want to get good at basketball and maybe play college basketball."
Oneda

"Ten years from now, I plan to have a family of my own. My family is going to be different. I'm not going to be like my mom and dad…..but no matter what, they will always be part of me."
Leeann

Miracle Eraser

If I could use my Miracle Eraser to erase anything I wanted, I would ....

"If I could use my Miracle Eraser to erase anything I wanted, I would erase my low self-image so that I could be more confident in who I am! I would erase memories which are not so good and my family's pain right now."

"……...I would erase every pain that I've caused in anyone's life."
        Leeann

"……...I would erase disease. I've watched too many people die. People I loved. People that I ran to when everything was going wrong. Still they had to suffer till their death. They didn't deserve such punishment. Nobody does."
       TL

"……...I would erase bad words, racial remarks, and missing my brother."
       Chris

"……...I would erase anything I wanted. I would erase bad memories, my pimples, and my bad habits."
       Roy

Miracle Eraser

"If I could use my Miracle Eraser to erase anything, it would be the physical and sexual abuse that happened to me and my sister. I would also erase being separated from my dad and my mom from being an alcoholic."
Kristal

"…….erase my hurt and pain, the hatred and depression I have inside——to love and give me freedom to let someone in and let me trust someone again."
Crystal

"……...I would erase my pain."
Antonio

"……...I would not erase anything, because even the stuff that I have done that was bad has led me to something better and that will help me learn skills for later in life."
Marco

"……...I would erase being taken out of my home and the bad situation so I could stay...running away and making the bad choices I did…..my brothers and sisters (my family) being separated from me….the violence in the world and that has happened in my life…..my mom choosing to take the wrong path she did….."
Oneda

"……...I would erase the fact that I give my heart away too easily…....never give the most precious thing you have to anyone unless it is for real. Never give your heart away!"
Leeann

"Commit to the Lord whatever you do, and your plans will succeed."
Proverbs 16:3

(right) After a word of prayer, Kathy gets class started.

(left) Chaplain Angie explaining the process as the first pages are examined.

(right) Chaplain Angie answering questions and keeping focus on our vision—
our chapel.

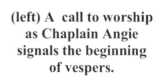

(left) A call to worship as Chaplain Angie signals the beginning of vespers.

Appendix

A. About our campus
    1. The Burlington Family Services Story
    2. Our Auxiliary

B. Spiritual Life and Related Information
    1. Spiritual Life Committee
    2. Order of Good Shepherds
    3. Resident Council
    4. Resident Council Membership Info
    5. Chapel Floor Plans and Specifications
    6. Say Yes To Kids

> "Use hospitality one to another
> without grudging.
> As every man hath received the gift, even
> so minister the same one to another, as good
> stewards of the manifold grace of God."
> 1 Peter 4:9, 10

THE BURLINGTON FAMILY SERVICES STORY

Burlington United Methodist Family Services, Inc., was founded in 1913 by Dr. F. L. Baker, a Burlington physician who also managed the original facilities, and Mr. F. C. Rollman, a Justice of the Peace, Notary, and Postmaster of Elk Garden. The original house, known as **The Star of Hope Child Refuge**, was purchased from Mrs. Mae Leatherman with a gift given by Mr. G. S. Kitzmiller and deeded to a Board of Trustees as an orphanage. From its earliest days, operating funds have been obtained through personal, business, church, and organizational donations. A part of today's funding also comes as purchase-of-service fees from state government. Fund raising and other supportive endeavors are conducted on an on-going basis by the Public Relations, Development, and Marketing Department that was founded in 1988.

Mr. William H. Barger, a Keyser newspaper publisher and editor, assumed management in 1933. In December 1949, an agreement was negotiated with Bishop Lloyd C. Wicke, and the West Virginia Annual Conference of the Methodist Episcopal Church assumed ownership and operation. The name was changed to the Methodist Children's Home on March 17, 1950.

In 1963, what is now called Collins Center was constructed as a girls' cottage. The Kitzmiller Cottage was built in 1965. What is now the Craig House Girls' Group Home was constructed in 1967 as the administrator's residence. It was renovated to accommodate six girls and staff in 1980. The Compton Administration Building was finished in 1969. Fifty-seven years after the original Star of Hope House was purchased, it was razed in 1970. In 1973, the Rees-Headlee Cottage was built, and the Keyser Boys' Group Home, the first off-campus facility, was purchased and renovated in 1985.

Each October the Children's Home Campus is the site of the famous Burlington Old Fashioned Apple Harvest Festival. Started by the Burlington United Methodist Family Services Auxiliary in 1974 as a fund raising project for Burlington, the Festival has grown to become a major attraction and community-wide event attracting an estimated 40,000 visitors each year. The Auxiliary, an integral part of Burlington's ministry, received national recognition in 1982 as **Volunteer Group of the Year** among all United Methodist Health and Welfare Ministries.

The year 1985 also marked the beginning of an intentional effort to address the "preventive" side of the service spectrum with the establishment of our first community-based services. Today, these services consist of specialized foster care, transitional living, family preservation, truancy diversion, and other services with offices located in Keyser, Grafton, Beckley, Scott Depot, and Petersburg, West Virginia, and Oakland, Maryland.

In 1989, United Methodist Child Placement Services merged with Burlington bringing back a ministry of adoption and birth parent counseling services, which had started at Burlington some 30 years earlier.

Burlington is nationally-accredited by the United Methodist Association of Health and Welfare Ministries as an **EAGLE** organization, a mark of distinction in services and quality. The **EAGLE** accreditation was first presented to Burlington after an intensive self-study and peer review process in 1991 and was renewed in 1996. In 1997, Burlington also achieved accreditation by the Council on Accreditation (COA) of Services for Families and Children, Inc.

In March 1994, Burlington received a national recognition award from among 400 organizations who are members of the United Methodist Health and Welfare Association. The award was the highest presented by the Association and designated Burlington as *"Organization of the Year."*

Burlington assumed possession of the campus of the former Beckley Child Care Center in 1995 at the invitation of the Beckley Board of Directors. After an extensive renovation, state licenses were obtained to provide residential treatment services and a full range of community based services to southern West Virginia beginning in 1997.

Burlington is now one of the largest and most diverse infant, child, youth, and family service organizations in West Virginia. Wherever you travel across this state and in many parts of the country, you will find a supportive church and private constituency who know and believe in Burlington's mission. This is an organization much larger than its staff. Many friends express loyalty and love continually through gifts and volunteer services.

Now we are entering another exciting phase of our growth-----the building of our own campus chapel. This venture began from a request of the resident council, a group formed by the campus chaplain Rev. Angela Cosner, for residents to have their own place to pray and worship. Often, during a time of struggle or stress, the residents would ask Rev. Cosner to walk with them to Burlington Union Church so they could gather at the altar and pray. During summer vespers, services would sometimes be moved off campus to the church because of rain. Increasingly, the residents felt the need for a place of worship for themselves, and the team of Burlington United Family Services listened to the desires of the young people they serve. Plans were drawn and decisions were made. Through the continued support of residents, staff, management, and volunteers, the chapel will stand as a testament to the growing faith of all who believe in the mission and vision of our total campus ministry.

Our Auxiliary

Over the years, our campus auxiliary has truly been a cornerstone of our children's ministry. Its importance and effect upon the lives of each resident cannot be overstated or overlooked. Simply put, it has been an integral part of our success and a constant source of support and encouragement since its inception. The meeting from which our auxiliary grew was held in Parsons on October 27, 1969, and was called by the administrator at the time, Rev. Andrew Agnew. The membership was 221 and the group's treasury balance was reported to be $256. From that humble beginning has grown an army of present day volunteers that do everything from peel apples to provide building funds for the campus projects.

The first president to be elected and serve the organization was Mrs. Donald Kiser, and the group began the first of its tasks—assuming the $400 debt of the tv tower on campus. During that first year, the tower debt was paid and water coolers were installed in each of the cottages. The next year, the auxiliary held its first open house. They met and agreed to purchase a lawn mower and furnish new curtains for two of the cottages as well as purchase new sleds and Bibles for each resident. By 1972, a third cottage was being built on campus, and the auxiliary agreed to furnish the living room of the cottage and to supplement a scholarship fund which had been established for residents with a portion of their membership fees. With much to be done—and willing hearts and hands to do it—the decision was made to look for additional resources to support the campus activities and programs, and it was decided to begin an **Old Fashioned Apple Harvest Festival.** After much careful planning, the first festival was help on October 18-20, 1974. The rest, as they say, is truly history!

The annual **Old Fashioned Apple Harvest Festival** has grown to become one of the most widely-known festivals in the tri-state area, drawing as many as 40,000 visitors to our tiny community each October. Through the support of the auxiliary and its army of willing souls, anywhere one looks on campus can be seen the result of their efforts. Over the years the auxiliary members have truly shown themselves to be servants of God's children, working tirelessly to meet the needs that are presented to them. Among other things, the auxiliary has purchased vans and cars, replaced furniture, installed kitchen cabinets, added closets, replaced curtains, provided scholarship funds, purchased clothing, provided microwaves, provided exercise equipment, and made the publication of this book possible—as it continues to extend a listening ear and a willing hand for the needs of the children.

Spiritual Life Committee

Mission Statement
The mission of Burlington United Methodist Family Services' Spiritual Life Program is to share the love and grace of God in Jesus Christ with all who come into our care and contact so they may gain faith awareness and experience wholeness of body, mind, and soul.

The campus Spiritual Life Committee is an important part of the total treatment program of our youth ministry. To meet the spiritual needs of our clients, opportunities for worship and spiritual growth are offered on the campus and in the communities where our services are provided. The Spiritual Life Committee recognizes the special obligations in developing "the whole person." Therefore, the goals of our program are to aid the residents in developing and successfully maintaining a relationship to a religious faith, a relationship to the world, a relationship to others, and a relationship to self. Membership on the committee is comprised of up to twenty members: at least three trustees, up to eleven staff, two representatives from resident's council, and up to four other appointees. The committee meets at least four times a year. Rev. Angela Cosner, campus chaplain, serves as Spiritual Life Coordinator to give leadership to the program, coordinate resources, and ensure effective implementation to the program.

The Spiritual Life activities on our campus are far-reaching. Some examples of events and activities of the program include presentation of Bibles with individual orientation and guidance, grace at meals, encouraging church attendance of the residents, teach respect for other religions and cultures, conducting weekly Christian education classes in the units, having youth fellowship activities, holding vesper services, and sponsoring service opportunities such as walk-a-thons to cultivate a spirit of giving and caring for others. Our chaplain visits residents and staff during illness and offers support during grief and tragedies. The Spiritual Life Committee plans and presents events and programs during religious and cultural holidays. The Rainbow Choir appears at various local churches and annual at Apple Harvest. They have also entertained our church officials at annual conference as well as district conference.

Order of Good Shepherds

Celebrating Ministry
In the Workplace

Holding God's People in Our Hearts
Hearing God's Call to Care
Sharing Our Gifts with Others

Our Burlington campus joins various sites across the country as a local chapter of the United Methodist Association's Order of Good Shepherds. Our chaplain, Rev. Angela Cosner, was introduced to the program when she attended a recent UMA conference. As part of her campus Spiritual Life program, Pastor Angie began introducing the idea and helping to organize chapters of the program for our employees on our Burlington campus and at other sites across the state. She continues to serve as an Order of Good Shepherds facilitator and does follow-up presentations for the local chapters to help encourage membership and to provide support for their efforts.

The Order of Good Shepherds is a voluntary program for employees who seek to connect their faith and their work. The mission of the Order is to recognize, affirm, and nurture the connection between employees' faith and their ministry in the workplace.

Benefits to employees, employers, and those the participants serve are endless. It enables healing and caring ministries to be spirit-centered, faith-based, and Wesleyan-focused as it enhances the quality of care provided to clients. It recognizes and nurtures the call of the employees and the variety of gifts they bring to the workplace. It offers an opportunity for employees to participate in an on-going connection group for self-discovery, education, faith-sharing, and service. In addition, it provides a national network of people who are living their faith and witnessing to others daily as they minister to the needs of those they serve.

Resident Council:
Developing Leadership and Responsibility

Resident Council provides positive peer leadership to our campus and allows the residents to identify and address issues they encounter each day. On Resident Council, students are given an active voice in campus affairs, and they take their job very seriously! In addition to serving their peers on Resident Council, two members are also chosen to serve as voting members on the Spiritual Life Committee and the Human Rights Committee.

Under Pastor Angie's guidance, the Resident Council plans and directs numerous campus activities. Each summer they plan Rec Week, a week of structured recreation activities. The council chooses the activities, sets the guidelines for their peers, and determine the behaviors that are desirable and those unacceptable for the participants during the week. They particularly enjoy competing and challenging the members of staff as they participate in the activities. Once the activities and rules are set, the representatives take the information back to their respective units and the information is discussed in the unit's community group meeting. The week's activities are closed with a talent show each year, and the residents choose a mission project to support.

Resident Council is active throughout the year. They plan fall and winter activities for their peers, usually a ski trip in the winter and a trip to Kings Dominion in the summer or fall. They also plan the Volunteer Appreciation Program to honor those who help make their activities possible. Each year the Spring Shower honoring the graduates is on the agenda, as well as plans to attend Ash Wednesday service and an activity planned in conjunction with the West Virginia School for the Deaf and Blind in Romney. One of the favorite activities the group plans each year is the Christmas play. This year when the students rated the activities, it was clearly the favorite. Each resident evaluating it gave it a 10. With results such as these, we are clearly doing something right!

Burlington United Methodist Family Services, Inc. Residents' Council

Purpose
Burlington United Methodist Family Services, Inc., has formulated a Residents' Council whose mission is *"to provide a voice in the leadership of activities that affect our lives."*

Membership
Membership on the council consists of a minimum of two residents and one staff person per unit/group home. The members are evaluated for leadership ability and peer interaction each quarter due to turnover rate of staff and discharge of residents from the program. Candidates are nominated by peers and approved by each unit's treatment team.

Objectives
- To establish an appropriate grievance protocol for residents in the program;
- To act as a collaborative group with a voice to bring about change;
- To assist with planning and coordinating recreation, leisure, and other activities; and
- To provide peer representation at agency planning and development meetings.

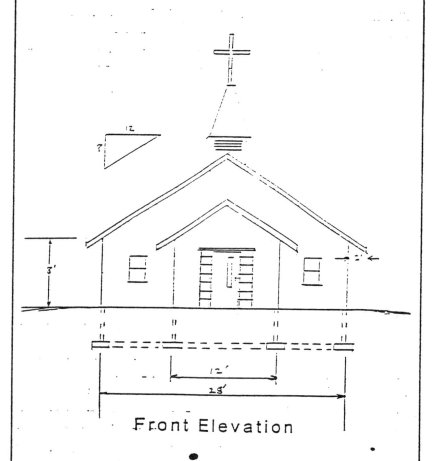

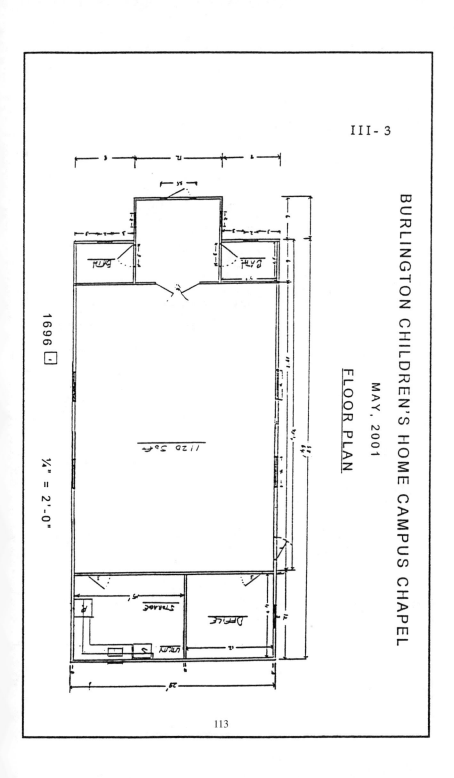

BURLINGTON CAMPUS CHAPEL
BUILDING SPECIFICATIONS

May, 2001

❑	Poured concrete foundation	10" x 20" footer
❑	Floor Joists	2" x10", 16" O. C.
❑	Subfloor	¾" plywood or equivalent
❑	Exterior Studding	2" x 6", 16" O. C.
❑	Interior Studding	2" x 4", 16" O. C.
❑	Roof Trusses	8:12 pitch, vaulted (6:12), 2" x 6." 2' O. C.
❑	Roofing Material	Metal roofing system, 1 x 6 roofers
❑	200 AMP Electrical Service	Wired to Code
❑	Heating, Cooling	Electric
❑	Windows	Vinyl, insulating glass, or equivalent
❑	Exterior Doors	Heavy-duty metal, insulated with glass insert
❑	Interior Doors	Solid, fire-rated as appropriate, birch finish, or equivalent
❑	Insulation	R-31 ceilling, R-19 walls, R-19 floor over crawl space
❑	Interior Walls	½" drywall - finished, painted
❑	Interior Ceiling System	Rustic wood, decorative beams
❑	Kitchenette	Includes wall, base cabinets with countertop, sink (double bowl), refrigerator, household-type electric stove, vented range hood
❑	Water Heater	40 gallon electric
❑	Floors	Carpet (office), Vinyl (kitchen, vestibule, bathrooms), Hardwood (sanctuary).
❑	Plumbing	Installed to code
❑	Water	From Craig House or new public service district
❑	Sewage	Tied into existing campus sewage treatment system
❑	Exterior Sheathing	½" OSB or equivalent
❑	Exterior Siding	Log siding – pine or equivalent
❑	Soffit, Facia	Vinyl and Aluminum as Appropriate
❑	Steeple	Donor to Supply
❑	Fire Safety System	Installed per NFPA Code

Say Yes To Kids

At Burlington United Methodist Family Services, Inc., our doors and our hearts have been open to countless abused children and at-risk youth for years, and we hope to continue being that place of shelter for years to come.

We all know that the children are our future. Enriching the life of a child will provide a better future for each of us. We wish to express our most heartfelt thanks to those of you who faithfully support our ministry. We daily see the miracles you have helped make possible. Many lives have been changed because of the gifts of you————our partners. God's blessings to each of you!

Foundation Office
Burlington United Methodist Family Services, Inc.
145 Southern Drive
Keyser, WV 26726
(304) 788-1953

B. Some Resources Used In Class

Included here are several handouts and writing prompts that were used as part of the curriculum for our creative arts class. We opened each class session with a freewrite using a transparency on the overhead to trigger the thoughts and reactions. Some examples we used were a dog lying with its head on the window sill as if watching and longing for someone; a hand reaching for the doorknob with the door slightly open, as if entering or leaving; a girl walking through a field of wheat, leaving a trail behind her—as if thinking about a problem—with a picture of an old house and a young man in the background.

For our groupthink activity, we used an overhead of Langston Hughes's poem "Dreams," and we talked about the visualization when comparing objects using similes and metaphors. We then took topics our students deal with often—faith, family, anger, love , life, etc.——and completed them as a group activity, discussing each one as we felt it to be necessary. This was quite effective done as a transparency on the overhead.

During each activity, we gave the opportunity for the students to share with the group. The ideas and discussion that followed was often surprising and enlightening. Staff members participated in the activities, which served as role models for the residents.

We used a combination of activities. Some very structured, such as the form poem on age included here. Other activities were designed to be more creative, such as writing from the point of view of an object with which the students spend a lot of time (see p. 53) .

Our activities and discussions were design to prompt thought and growth——and healing—within each participant.

☺ *(Please note: Rev. Angela Cosner and Kathy Johnson will be using some of the following material in other books and curriculum guides currently being developed and compiled by Rainbow Publications, which will specialize in holistic teaching material for at-risk youth.)*

Note: Effective when used with the poem
"Dreams" by Langston Hughes and done
as a group activity.

Group think

Anger is a (like a) _____ that _____.

1. _____ that_____
2. _____ that _____.
3. _____ that _____.

Goals are (like)_____ that_____.

1._____ that _____.
2._____ that _____.
3._____ that_____.

A family is (like a)_____ that _____.

1. _____ that_____.
2. _____ that _____.
3. _____ that_____.

Emotions are _____ that_____.

1. _____ that_____.
2. _____ that_____.
3. _____ that_____ >

Name:_____.

Creative Arts Class

Life is a _____that_____.
1.
2.
3.
4.
5.

A friend is a _____that_____.
1.
2.
3.
4.
5.

Faith is a _____that_____.
1.
2.
3.
4.
5.

Love is a _____that_____.
1.
2.
3.
4.
5.

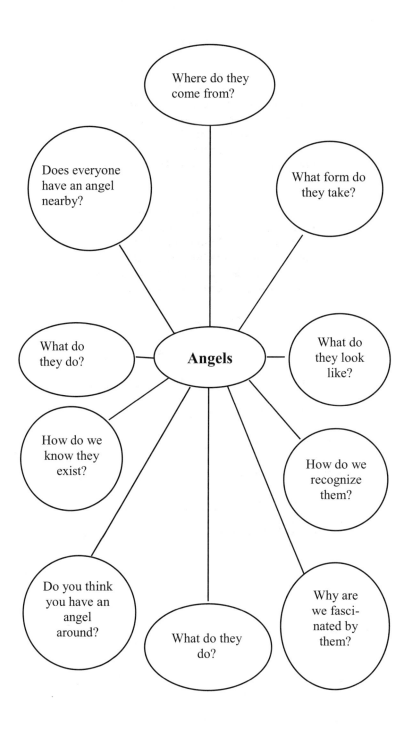

Name_____

Your age
A year of (put two things here)
I'm looking forward to (one thing)
I'm excited about (one thing)
I'm nervous about (one thing)
And I fear (one thing)
All in all, life is (or can be) (finish sentence)

Seventeen
A year of joys and sorrows
I'm looking forward to getting out of school.
I'm excited about dating Tony.
I'm nervous about starting my new job.
And I fear that no one will love me.
All in all, life can be very stressful at times.

Your response:

_____(age)

A year of _____and _____

I'm looking forward to _____.

I'm excited about _____.

I'm nervous about_____.

And I fear_____.

All in all, life is (can be)_____.

Responsive Writing Topics (list A)

I like to write because.....
It sounds crazy, but.......
Today I realized that......
I looked everywhere for _____ and found it........
When I have time, I like to............
I have this unforgettable dream.........
The hardest thing I have ever done...
The most meaningful thing I have ever done.....
The worst thing to wait for is......
I get my best ideas when......
When I get older, I am thinking about......
Ten years from now I can imagine myself............
The best advice I've ever gotten was............because...
I think a true friend is............
I am proud of myself when..........
I am disappointed in myself when....
Someone I really respect is .._____...because......
One of my most cherished memories is.......
My favorite special place is............because
Today I feel very..............
A time someone did something that I respected was...........
I feel happy when..............
I feel sad when..............
If I were rich I'd...............
I am a good friend because I...............
I am working on...........
One thing I have always wondered about is............
You wouldn't understand what it is like to ....
I have learned to relax by ....
My favorite time of the day is...........
A book I read that touched me is......
If I could write a book, it would be about..........
We learn from mistakes, and one time I.......
My favorite food is ..._____because..........
I am frightened by.........
I am encouraged ......

Responsive Writing Topics (B)

- Write about some of the things that make you feel happy.
- Write a poem that starts with "Joy is….."
- Write about what you do when you get discouraged or scared or worried……
- Write about "quiet."
- Write about what you like and/or dislike about school.
- Write about what you value most in life.
- Write about what you need in life to feel good
- Write about what makes you laugh
- Write about what makes you cry
- Write a poem that begins with "God is……."
- Write a letter to someone about something important that you need to tell him or her
- Write a poem about your greatest blessing
- Write a poem that begins or ends with "I am grateful for.."
- Create a cartoon character that represents you
- Write a prayer in the form of a poem or a free verse
- Write your own Code of Honor-----5-10 rules to live by
- Make a "Top Ten List" of reasons to Believe or Reasons to Set Goals for Ourselves
- Choose an object or possession that is important to you and explain why
- There is an old saying that the road to (the bad place—you know what I mean!) is paved by good intentions. What is the road to Heaven paved with? Explain.
- Explain what your greatest gift or talent is and how you use it or don't use it.
- Write about something that you have done that you are proud of
- Write about something that you wished you should have done and didn't
- Write about a special friend you have or have had
- Write about your first day going somewhere, where you were nervous or worried about what to do
- Describe someone who impressed you the first time you met or saw them and why
- Describe someone you look up to and why
- If you could choose a quote to represent your life, what would it be and why.

My Cloak

Go over definition of "Cloak"
Webster's definition of "cloak":

N. 1. A loose outer garmet. 2. That which conceals; a blind; disguise; mask. V. 1. To cover with a cloak or mask 2. To hide or conceal.

Discuss how we conceal ourselves from others or the kinds of things we conceal. Have students to create their own "cloak". It could be a cloak of emotions, a cloak of experiences, a cloak of dreams, a cloak of fears, a cloak of friends, a cloak of goals, a cloak of family, or any combination of these.

Students who like to draw can draw their cloak. (as in example on overhead.) Students who choose to write can describe what they conceal. Students may choose to just use descriptive words and phrases for their cloak.

Students may either draw the face as they choose, leave it blank, or add the face as they want to represent it.